DAILY LIFE ON T

WAGON TRAIL

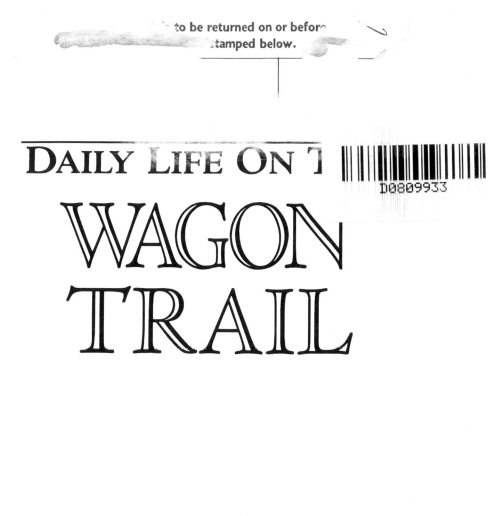

Paul Erickson

Heinemann
LIBRARY

First published in Great Britain by Heinemann Library,
Halley Court, Jordan Hill, Oxford OX2 8EJ,
a division of Reed Educational and Professional Publishing Ltd.

Heinemann is a registered trademark of Reed Educational & Professional Publishing Limited.

OXFORD MELBOURNE AUCKLAND
JOHANNESBURG BLANTYRE GABORONE
IBADAN PORTSMOUTH NH (USA) CHICAGO

03 02 01 00 98
10 9 8 7 6 5 4 3 2 1

ISBN 0 431 04241 1
This title is also available in a hardback library edition (ISBN 0 600 57987 5).

British Library Cataloguing in Publication Data
Erickson, Paul
Daily life on the wagon trail
1.Pioneers - West (U.S.) - Social conditions - Juvenile
literature 2.Frontier and pioneer life - West (U.S.) -
Juvenile literature 3. Oregon Trail - Juvenile literature
I.Title
978í.02

Printed in Hong Kong

Conceived and produced by Breslich & Foss Limited, London
Series Editor: Laura Wilson
Art Director: Nigel Osborne
Design: Sally Stockwell
Illustrations: Ben Warner, Peter Owen
Cover illustration: Andrew Beckett
Photography: Nigel Bradley

CONTENTS

Going West

I n the 1840s the United States doubled in size (*see map right*). By either negotiation, war or purchase, it acquired most of Oregon, Texas, California and the American Southwest. There was a great desire to expand into the little known territories of the West, and several

Right: *Western Expansion of the United States by 1853.*

Above: *Map of the Oregon Trail.*

people went out to explore the region and came back with reports of rich soil and good opportunities for farmers. Interest in the West grew, until it was said that "if hell were in the West, Americans would cross heaven to get there". Newspaper editors spoke of the nation's wish to make the United States stretch "from sea to shining sea". "Oregon Fever" was just one part of this western expansion. According to the "boosters" who encouraged people to move West, Oregon was a paradise "flowing with milk and honey". It was even said that pigs ran around ready cooked with knives and forks sticking in them so that anyone could have a slice!

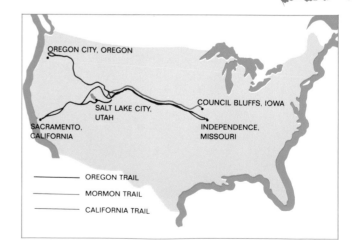

Above: *The three main trails West.*

THE RESOURCES OF CALIFORNIA AND THEIR DEVELOPMENT.

Above: *A gold pan.*

Left: *A "boosterist" poster showing the West as a paradise.*

Above: *James K Polk became President in 1844 because he promised Americans "All of Oregon or War!" In the early 1840s, part of Oregon still belonged to Great Britain.*

However, the journey West was difficult and dangerous. There were no railways or roads and the "overlanders" travelled in a wagon train made up of a line of wagons. The routes they took became known as the wagon trails. Despite the difficulties of crossing "the Great American desert", there were several reasons to go West. Some people, like the Mormons, wanted to be free to practise their religion; others, like the "Forty-Niners" of the 1849 California Gold Rush, hoped to find gold and get rich; and others, like those on the Oregon Trail, wanted to make better lives for themselves farming on the fertile land.

Most of the pioneers wanted to bring "civilization" with them: fashions and entertainments as well as laws, schools and colleges. They wanted to stay in touch with what was happening back East, no matter how different their new lives were.

THE FAMILY

The year is 1853, and the Larkin family are on their way to Oregon. For a journey of over 3,200 kilometres, lasting nearly five months, a covered wagon will be their home. Like so many other Americans, they have made the momentous decision to "emigrate", that is, to leave the settled states East of the Mississippi for a new and better life in the West.

HIRAM LARKIN

HETTY LARKIN

Above and right: *Books like Palmer's* Journal of Travels over the Rocky Mountains *and Horn's* Overland Guide *are Mr Larkin's favourite reading.*

Mr Larkin has thought very carefully before deciding to make the trip to Oregon. On his 110-acre farm in Indiana, he is able to provide for his family. As a land owner, he is certainly better off than a labourer, but he finds it hard to make a profit, and he is worried that the soil in Indiana is "worn out".

Hiram Larkin, age 35, is of Scots-Irish ancestry. Like his father and grandfather before him, he is a hard-working farmer. He did not get swept up in the first bout of "Oregon Fever" in the mid-1840s, but his views changed when he began to read reports of the trip and of the richness of the Oregon soil. Now he has sold his farm and stock back in Indiana and taken his family by steamboat to the "jumping-off point" of Independence, Missouri, where the emigrants meet up and make preparations before starting on their long overland trek.

Hetty Gilkey married Hiram Larkin when she was 18 years old. Now she is 33. Like Hiram, she comes from a farming family. Hetty did not want to leave Indiana at first, but she changed her mind after the Donation Land Act was passed in 1850. This law cut the amount of land an Oregon settler could claim from 640 acres to 320 acres, but allowed him to claim 320 acres for his wife. Hetty liked the idea of owning land herself. She helped her husband to save money for the trip, and borrowed from her brother.

6

THE CHILDREN

Rachel (14), Abraham (10), Rebecca (7)
and Margaret (3)

At the time of their emigration to Oregon, Hiram and Hetty Larkin have four children – fewer than most farming families of that time. A fifth child (born between Rachel and Abraham) died of scarlet fever when he was only two years old.

The eldest child Rachel is now nearly 15. Since having scarlet fever as a little girl Rachel has been sickly, and her mother worries that the trip to Oregon will be too much for her heart. Her father, however, points out that the trip West has restored many sick people to good health.

Abraham, or Abe, and Rebecca are both thrilled to be travelling to Oregon and cannot wait to get started. Little Margaret, who has just turned three, is too young to understand quite what is happening. She clings to her mother's skirts and seems completely bewildered by all the changes going on around her.

MATTHEW BELKNAP

Matthew, or Matt, Belknap is an 18-year-old orphan from St Louis. After his parents died in a cholera epidemic, Matt lived with an uncle, but ran away to Independence because he was badly treated. Now Matt has been hired by Hiram Larkin. In return for "a man's work", which will be mainly hunting and looking after cattle, Matt will join the Larkin household for the trip to Oregon.

THE WAGON

"The wagon looks so nice, with its white cover. It is plenty high enough for me to stand straight under the roof. Once it starts rolling, with everything packed away ship-shape, it will be a prairie schooner indeed!" Mrs Larkin's Diary

All Mr Larkin's guidebooks say that the key to a successful journey to Oregon is a good wagon. The wagon must be strong, in order to carry a load of perhaps 900 kg over rough and mountainous country, but it must also be light, in order not to strain the oxen pulling it. Rather than risk using the family's rickety old farm wagon, Mr Larkin decided to buy

Above: *Wagon trains waiting to begin the journey.*

a new wagon in Independence. At $110 (£65), it is the most expensive thing he has bought for the trip. Even Mrs Larkin is pleased with it. She has decided to call it "Hoosier Home" because the Larkins come from Indiana and people from that state are sometimes called "hoosiers".

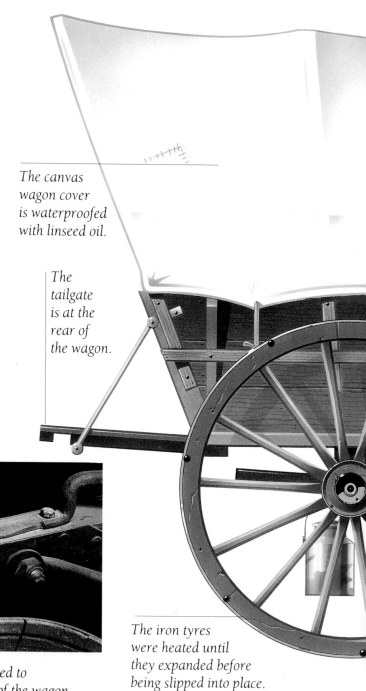

The canvas wagon cover is waterproofed with linseed oil.

The tailgate is at the rear of the wagon.

The iron tyres were heated until they expanded before being slipped into place.

Above: *The cover is threaded through with a "puckering string" at each end, so that it can be opened and closed.*

Above: *Iron is used to strengthen parts of the wagon such as the axles and wheels.*

Left: *The wagons were parked in a circle at night to give protection from wolves, cattle thieves and the wind.*

Below: *The body of the wagon is a box 1 metre wide by 3 metres long.*

Bows made out of hickory wood were used to hold up the canvas.

The jockey box at the front of the wagon is used to sit on and to hold tools.

The oxen were harnessed to the wagon tongue.

The wheels have hubs of elm, spokes of oak and rims of ash, all firmly bolted together. They are greased with tallow and tar to make them run smoothly.

Left: *The wheels are fixed to the axles with iron bolts and pins.*

INSIDE THE WAGON

The Larkins' wagon is not a travelling house like a modern caravan, it is more of a storage space. It is loaded with provisions for the long journey and for fitting out a new farmstead in Oregon. The tools that Mr Larkin will need for farming are strapped to the sides, and spare parts for the wagon are slung

Above: *A large trunk stowed in the bottom of the wagon keeps family treasures safe during the journey.*

Above: *Barrels, rope, iron pots, tin plates, ladles, nails, a chair and a rifle will all be needed in Oregon, as well as on the wagon train.*

underneath. Inside, there is a leather trunk filled with medicines, a bottle of matches tightly corked to keep out moisture, the big family Bible and other special treasures carried from Indiana. One wooden box contains the pots, pans and cutlery that the Larkins will need for the trip. Another box, carefully stowed away, is filled with rolls of cloth, good linen and the family's "best clothes", which will not come out again until the Larkins arrive in Oregon. Yet another box contains plant cuttings, since Mr Larkin hopes to have an orchard on his new farm. Mrs Larkin watches as the men load the wagon to make sure that the more precious things are tucked out of harm's way.

Above: *A scythe and hoe are tied to the side of the wagon. A tin pitcher holds grease for the wheel axles.*

10

Above: *Hardtack or "pilot bread" could be kept for several months.*

Blankets, pillows and featherbeds are wrapped up in canvas groundsheets. Tents, poles, ropes and stakes are stacked to one side of the wagon, propped in place by a few pieces of furniture. Everyday clothing hangs from hooks fixed to the hickory bows, while pockets in the canvas walls hold cord, small guns and Mrs Larkin's sewing things and toiletries. A lantern hangs overhead along with a ready shotgun.

Food for the Journey

Strong canvas sacks, their seams well stitched by Mrs Larkin back in Indiana, are now filled up with the huge amounts of food recommended in the guidebooks: 45 kg of flour for each adult, 30 kg of bacon, 15 kg of "pilot bread" or hardtack, beans, rice, coffee, sugar, dried fruits, baking soda, vinegar – all bought from the stores in Independence.

Above: *A calico blouse, a cotton apron and other finery will remain packed until arrival in Oregon.*

Below: *Eggs, china and other fragile items are packed in barrels of cornmeal.*

Communications

Mrs Larkin packs her pen away carefully. Like many overlanders, she will keep a diary and write letters to relatives back East. Letters can be left for posting at various places along the way. For other messages, there is a "roadside telegraph" or "bone express": messages are left for the following wagon trains, posted on a cleft stick or scribbled on sun-bleached bones. Sometimes they give good advice, such as: "For God's sake do not taste this water. It is poisonous", but some pranksters leave misleading messages to confuse other travellers.

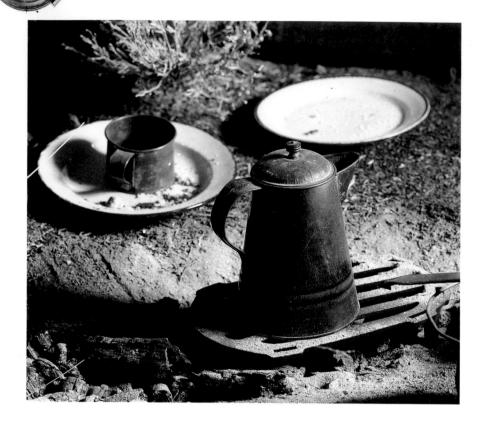

Left: *Once the fire is lit, Mrs Larkin roasts the coffee beans over it, before grinding them. Then she puts the pot on the fire to boil.*

Right: *An overlander's breakfast might be johnnycake, bacon and coffee.*

DAYBREAK

A t 4 am the night watch fire their guns to let everyone know that it is daybreak. Quickly, the overlanders pull on their boots or shoes, throw a few garments over the clothes they have slept in, and set about their morning tasks.

Mrs Larkin cooks the breakfast. First, she has to make a fire. A steady wind is always blowing across the prairies, so she must dig a shallow trench. Then she needs to find some fuel.

On the high plains a wagon train might travel for days without seeing a single tree, but the pioneers soon discovered that dried buffalo droppings, or "buffalo chips", made a clean, hot fire with little smoke or smell. In the mountains, dead sage brush would do instead.

Even with her trench filled with fuel, Mrs Larkin often has difficulty lighting the fire. Sometimes she resorts to sprinkling the fuel with gunpowder.

Above: *A mill for grinding coffee beans.*

Breakfast

Pancakes are breakfast favourites as they need only flour, water, baking soda and a frying pan. Mrs Larkin often bakes bread in a dutch oven, using risen dough that she prepared the evening before. On other days she makes soda biscuits, muffins or cornmeal johnnycakes. Beans, well greased with bacon and slowly simmered through the night in the ashes of the fire, are a popular breakfast dish, as is fried meat, which is served with a gravy made of pan drippings and flour. The overlanders like to begin the day with a hearty meal.

Coffee is the trail thirst-quencher, served at every meal. The overlanders rarely drink plain water since it is usually muddy or polluted and tastes so disgusting that sometimes even the animals refuse it. It is only when the dirty water's taste is disguised by the strong flavour of coffee that the overlanders and their animals can drink it.

Above: *Cast-iron frying pans and a long-handled pan for making popcorn.*

"There is a great scarcity of wood, and we are compelled to cook our food with buffalo chips. This has caused many of the ladies to act very cross, but necessity is a great leveller, and now we all must search for them."
Mrs Larkin's Diary

Above and below: *Carefully designed portable canteens like these could carry plates, bowls, cutlery, jars for sugar and salt, and larger items such as flasks for vinegar.*

HITCHING UP THE WAGON

W hile Mrs Larkin is preparing breakfast, the men of the party round up the livestock. The riding horses are close at hand. They have been hobbled to the wagons during the night in case they are stolen by Indians. The cattle, however, have been left free to graze where they like, and some of them have wandered far from the camp in search of the tastiest grass.

Overlanders used different animals to carry their luggage or pull their wagons or carts. Farming families like the Larkins usually chose oxen to pull the wagon the 3,200 km journey, since these animals are very strong. However, men bound for the California goldfields often chose a pack-train of mules which could go faster than a covered wagon, even when carrying panniers (*see below*) filled with heavy supplies.

Left: *Overlanders bound for the goldfields would carry their supplies in a pair of panniers strapped over a mule's back.*

Right: *On hard or rocky trails iron shoes protected the oxen's feet.*

14

Farming families did use mules for pulling their wagons, as they were tough, relatively speedy, and could survive on cottonwood bark, but the vast majority preferred oxen. Although oxen were slower than mules, they fared much better in muddy conditions and could survive on little food. Most of the overlanders used oxen on their farms back East and were experienced at handling them. Besides that, oxen were about half the price of mules.

After the cattle have been driven into the circle of wagons and sorted out, Mr Larkin yokes up his team of six oxen. While many overlanders used oxen from their old farmsteads, Mr Larkin bought these in Independence. He wanted them to be fresh for the journey, and he also knew that oxen in Missouri were supposed to be cheap, and accustomed to eating the tough grasses of the prairie.

Like the Larkins, most overlanders have one or two saddle horses. However, horses were not used to pull the wagons until the later years of the trail because they could not work well with such poor feed.

In addition to their oxen, the Larkins have two dairy cows. Rachel and Abe have the task of milking them every morning and evening. In the evening the Larkin family drink the milk fresh with their supper, but in the morning Mrs Larkin puts the milk into a churn, which she hangs from the back of the wagon. On the trail she does not have time to make butter but without it even her tasty biscuits and pancakes are too dry to eat. Fortunately she has learned a shortcut. As the wagon bumps along, the milk is shaken so vigorously that large balls of butter will form with no hand-churning at all!

Above:
Wooden ox yoke.

Right: *One company of Mormons travelled with two-wheeled handcarts which they pulled themselves.*

Right: *Otto Sommer's painting of the Oregon trail,* Westward Ho!

Above: *With this folding pocket sundial and compass, the captain can tell both time and direction.*

ROLLING THE TRAIN

At 7am a bugle sounds. As the women bundle away the last of the cookware, the men shout commands to their teams. "Roll the wagons!" calls the captain of the wagon train. The first wagon moves out of the camp, and soon the company has spread out across the prairie in a growing cloud of dust.

There are 60 families in the Larkins' wagon train. Some of these are old friends from Franklin County, Indiana, with whom the Larkins have been sharing travel plans for many months. There is a larger party from Illinois and there are assorted smaller groups from Missouri.

Even after the trail has become well-worn, few overlanders set off alone, preferring the support and security of a large group. Together, they make up a sort of village on wheels with men of all trades amongst the travellers. Like a village, the wagon train needs some rules, and meetings were held to elect a captain and some men to help him.

Above: *The pepperbox pistol was named after its black gunpowder.*

One early party even worked out a miniature government system with its own laws and courts. When the people chosen to be in charge of it refused to do lowly chores like guard duty, the ordinary "citizens" soon put a stop to their government!

Above: *In a wagon train, just as in the army, a bugle announced the major moments of the day.*

"We have elected Captain Bonner, of Weston, Missouri, to lead our company. The Illinois men might have preferred one of their own, but even they must admit that he is an expert with a bullwhip and handles the cattle very well."
Mr Larkin

Below: *The captain's spyglass, pipe and a fold-away knife for carving and whittling.*

The Captain

James J Bonner is captain of the Larkins' wagon train. A man of great experience, he has crossed the plains in both directions and knows the trail quite well. The company have chosen him instead of hiring a professional guide. Captain Bonner is responsible for all the major decisions about the wagon train: the route they will travel, the time for starting and stopping each day, the site where they will camp for the night, the site for the midday "nooning" (*see page 29*), the posting of guards and the daily rotation of the wagons. Rotation was necessary because no one wanted to be at the very end of a dusty wagon train every day!

Captain Bonner is worried because there has been a lot of rain. Although this means that there will be a good supply of grass for the animals, the swollen streams and mud will slow down the wagons. The party will need to make good time to get through the mountain passes to Oregon before they are blocked by snow. If they fail, they will have to spend the winter on the eastern side of the Blue Mountains.

ON THE TRAIL

With no springs or cushioned seats, the Larkins' wagon is far too uncomfortable to ride in. Most of the pioneers travelled the 3,200 kilometres of the Oregon trail on foot. If it rained, they simply put on oilskin ponchos or unfurled umbrellas and marched on. They did not have to walk fast, however, since the wagons lumbered along at the rate of only two or three kilometres an hour. Children who got tired might hitch a short ride on the wagon tongue. Sick people who had to ride in the wagon were put on featherbeds and padded round with pillows to relieve the worst of the jolting.

Mr Larkin walks alongside his oxen, shouting commands like "gee" (go right) and "haw" (go left). He carries a bullwhip which he cracks over their heads to tell them which way to go, and sometimes he uses it to flick flies away from their ears, but he never hits them with it. The pioneers considered it very bad to strike the oxen. Like many pioneer farmers Mr Larkin has given his oxen names: Dick, Tom, Hob, Sam, Tip and Dobie.

Above: *Men's boots had to be made large because there was no difference between the right and left boot.*

Below: *A man's felt hat, woollen undershirt and linen trousers.*

Above: *Matt Belknap likes to shave his beard whenever he gets the chance, in order to show off his dashing moustache. His shaving kit is very precious as it was one of the few things left to him by his father. Mr Larkin's beard, however, requires very little care, and it also gives him extra protection from the sun.*

Men's Clothes

Like most of the men in the wagon train, Mr Larkin wears the same clothes day in, day out. Even though it is midsummer, he wears a long-sleeved flannel shirt with a woollen undershirt beneath it and trousers of wool or linen, or a mixture of the two called "linsey-woolsey". Wool, as the guidebooks noted, offered good protection against the midday sun, the rain or any sudden changes in temperature. Denim, which is often associated with the West, came into wide use only after Levi Strauss introduced it in San Francisco in the 1870s. On Mr Larkin's feet are stout boots which give protection against snake bites. He also wears a broad-brimmed hat to keep the sun off his head and face – not having sunglasses or sunscreen, hats were very important to the overlanders.

Above: *A woman's blouse and sunbonnet.*

"Today mother became very angry with me for removing my sunbonnet. She pointed out to me some girls who did not wear bonnets, and as I did not want to look as brown as an Indian squaw, I put it on again, though it causes me no little discomfort."
Rachel Larkin's Diary

Women's Clothes

Mrs Larkin walks beside the wagon. Like her husband, she usually dresses in wool, though if the weather is very good she may wear checked gingham. Her skirt is hemmed an inch or two higher than would have been thought proper back East, to make it easier for her to walk over the rough ground. Mrs Larkin also wears an apron, partly to keep her dress clean, and partly because she, like everyone else at the time, considers the apron to be the right thing for a proper married woman – that is, a housewife – to wear. Although she does not have many clothes for the trip and has few chances for washing, Mrs Larkin makes a point of wearing a smarter, light-coloured apron on special occasions (*see page 36*). Her only regret is that she cannot starch it properly, as she would have back in Indiana. She always wears a sunbonnet to protect her face.

Rachel's clothing is much like her mother's. Because of her delicate health Rachel usually rides on a horse and she arranges her skirts carefully to cover her ankles. Rachel feels envious of the more daring women in the party, who are wearing "bloomers".

Left: *Mr Larkin bought this fine side-saddle for Rachel in St Louis.*

LANDMARKS ON THE TRAIL

F or the most part, the "trail" was exactly that: a rough, unimproved track. On difficult terrain, the wagons might follow the well-worn ruts left by previous travellers, some of which can still be seen today. On easier ground, the trail might spread out over a mile or more. There were a few places where army engineers or private businessmen had laid out proper roads by clearing away the trees and boulders. One of the best-known of these was a road made by Sam Barlow, who charged the overlanders a toll to use it. Most of them paid up willingly, as it saved them having to take the dangerous trail along the Columbia River.

Left: *Gulches or small valleys were a common problem for overlanders in the mountains. Deep gulches were hard to cross when they were dry, as this one is, but after heavy rain they were impassable.*

Above: *The Rocky Mountains.*

"Today we reached the foot of Chimney Rock. People say that it was thrust up out of the ground, but no one agrees how. One man, who had been a teacher back in Illinois, said that before the Flood the whole land had been as high as that rock." Rachel Larkin's Diary

Right: *The Larkin children are intrigued by the underground world of the prairie dogs, burrowing owls and rattlesnakes, like the snake shown here.*

Below: *A hand-drawn map of the trail from an overlander's notebook, with the names of rivers, mountains and stopping places such as forts and trading posts.*

Left: *As the Larkins get farther west, they spot many porcupines. The Indians use porcupine quills to decorate buckskin.*

The Larkins eagerly await their first glimpse of the trail's best-known landmarks, made famous by guidebook descriptions, magazine illustrations and paintings: the mountains at Scotts Bluff and Laramie Peak; the mountain called "Devils Gate" which was almost split in two by a deep notch; and Courthouse Rock and nearby Jail Rock, so called because their shapes reminded some early overlanders of the St Louis government buildings. There was also Soda Springs, where the bubbling waters tickled the travellers' noses and the bicarbonate deposits gave them new supplies of

Right: *Brown bears were found throughout the Northern Rockies.*

baking soda, and Steamboat Springs, whose puffs and snorts reminded overlanders of river travel back East. Independence Rock was called the "great register of the desert" and travellers climbed it to paint or carve their names. But the most famous of all was Chimney Rock (*see left*) a solitary 150 metre spire of sandstone and clay, rising above the flat prairie.

Above: *Chimney Rock, painted in 1837.*

TRIBES OF THE WEST

After they crossed the Missouri River, the overlanders were in Indian country. First they encountered the *Oto* and *Kansa* tribes, as well as some *Potawatomie* and *Kickapoo* Indians. These Indians lived in villages of tepees, and they bartered their vegetables for items like cloth and fish hooks. They also kept toll bridges over the deeply cut prairie creeks, which the overlanders found helpful but infuriating, as they had to pay to get across.

Left: A Klickitat *Indian. The* Klickitat *lived in the foothills of the Cascade Mountains and hunted in the Willamette Valley (see map on page 4).*

The *Pawnee* did some farming, but they were also horsemen and hunters. Their heads were shaved Mohican style, and they frequently fought with other plains tribes over hunting

territory. The *Lakota* (or *Dakota*) were a group of tribes whom the overlanders usually called the *Sioux*. Like the *Cheyenne* and *Arapaho*, the *Sioux* had been forced onto the plains in the eighteenth century by rival tribes. They soon became the most famous of the buffalo-hunting Indians of the plains.

The *Shoshone* Indians hunted, trapped and fished in the northern mountain regions. Like the *Nez Perce* and *Salish* (*Flatheads*), they were friendly to the overlanders, supplying them with fresh fish

Right: A tepee had a framework of 16 to 20 poles, lashed together near the top. This supported a semi-circular cover of buffalo hides which was held in place by 30-centimetre-long wooden pins slipped through the overlapping holes. Inside, the beds were made of pole frames padded with grass and covered with buffalo hides. Back rests made of woven willow were attached to turn them into seats in the daytime.

and berries and sometimes acting as guides. This was so well known that if any Indian in the region wanted to show goodwill to an overlander, he would say, "I Shoshone".

In the infertile regions of the Great Divide Basin, the *Utes* and related tribes had to live chiefly on roots and plants, which led overlanders bound for California to call them all *Digger* Indians. The *Cayuse, Umatilla, Chinook* and other fishing tribes whom the Oregon settlers met on the banks of the Columbia River were more prosperous.

"Today we saw some Nez Perce Indians and they looked very well. Father tried to say some words to them in their own language, which he got out of Mr Palmer's Guidebook, but they only laughed and so he walked away." Abe Larkin

Below: *Map of Indian territory in the mid-nineteenth century.*

Native American Crafts
Buffalo hides were used to make clothing, moccasins (a popular item for trade with overlanders), saddles for women (warriors used only a folded blanket held in place by a strap around the horse's belly), and parfleches, which were folding travelling pouches. In earlier times, these articles would have been decorated with geometrical designs fashioned from porcupine quills, but from about 1800 the Indians began to use porcelain and glass beads, obtained from white traders.

Right: *Fancy moccasins like these were probably only used for ceremonies. The beads would have been acquired in trade with the white travellers.*

23

INDIAN COUNTRY

In the 1840s and early 1850s, the Indians showed little interest in the overlanders. Sometimes the Indians demanded payments or goods, but often they were simply interested in making a profitable trade. What little bloodshed there was, generally involved small bands of young Indian braves out to impress their friends by stealing horses. More often than not, these youngsters were acting against the wishes of the chiefs, who had no desire to anger the travellers. Although the Indians were more a nuisance than a danger, the overlanders were wary. People like the Larkins had thought of Indians as "noble savages", but when they read stories about their cruelty in the "penny press" they were worried. The men who guarded the wagon train

"*This afternoon we passed a village of Sioux Indians. The women had moccasins and beads, which they wanted to trade for bread. Husband traded a big Indian a lot of pilot bread for a pair of moccasins, but after we started out he ran up making a big fuss and wanted them back. They had eaten some of the pilot bread and were not satisfied. We handed the moccasins to him in a hurry and drove away as fast as possible.*" Mrs Larkin's Diary

Above: *Native American weaving was of such high quality that it could be used for jars. The ladles are carved out of bone.*

at night would fire at any noise, and often ended up shooting each other. However, the Indians were much more interested in organizing raids against their traditional enemies than in attacking the overlanders. The Indians often used the rivers to mark the edges of their hunting grounds. As the wagon trains followed the rivers (*see page 32*), overlanders often met up with parties of Indians off to do battle. But they soon realized that, although young braves might steal their animals, the war parties would ignore them completely.

Left: *Native American tomb.*

The Indians' love of children was well
known. One diary tells of a mother
who put down her baby in some
tall grass in order to help her
husband lower their wagon down
a steep hill. She was horrified to
see a band of Indians gathering
round her child and ran towards
them. They stood back to let her
pass and she found her child lying
as she had left him.
The Indians had
been babysitting.

Above: *Native American dress
included a blanket and moccasins.
The saddle is covered with fur.*

By the mid-1850s, relations between Indians and overlanders had
worsened. A series of misunderstandings, and some trigger-happy
soldiers, led to the massacre of a *Sioux* village after the villagers had
been tricked by a flag of truce. This, and other similar conflicts, led
to over 30 years of "Indian Wars".

By 1890, the Indians' old way of life had been destroyed. The
buffalo, numbering perhaps twelve million in 1850, had been hunted
to near-extinction by the overlanders with their effective breech-
loading rifles (*see page 26*). White settlers were farming the prairies
and plains and the once mighty tribes of the West were
confined to reservations.

NEZ PERCE
WALLA WALLA
WASCO
SALISH (FLATHEAD)
CROW
NORTHERN CHEYENNE
SIOUX
PAIUTE
UTE
SHOSHONE
ARAPAHO
SHOSHONE
KICKAPOO
POTAWATOMIE
BANNOCK
SHOSHONE
KLAMATH
SHOSHONE
BANNOCK

Above: *Native American Reservations in 1890.*

Right: *This hunting
quiver, made of animal
pelts (skins), is decorated
with beads and red cloth.*

HUNTING

The prairies were known to be rich in game, and the overlanders counted on being able to hunt for food. They were well prepared: each adult male was expected to

Above: *The cartridges in this belt were used in the buffalo hunters' rifles.*

have at least one rifle and a revolver. Additional supplies included shotguns, bullet moulds, lead, gunpowder and assorted knives. The guidebooks

advised overlanders to carry these weapons in case they were attacked by Indians, but in fact they were far more often used for hunting. Each morning, the captain would send out a party of sharp-shooters, such as Matt Belknap, to hunt.

During the first stages of the journey, the hunters seldom came back with anything bigger than rabbits, prairie chickens, pheasants and other small birds and animals. But as they travelled farther west, they could hope for elk, antelope, bighorn sheep and, best of all, buffalo.

Techniques for hunting buffalo varied. Before they got horses and firearms, the Indians would often stampede a herd over a precipice and then finish them off with bows and arrows. A hunter armed with a rifle might walk to within a few yards of a buffalo and, if it did not catch his scent, he could fire off round after round of bullets.

Above: *A buffalo hunter's kit, with a warm jacket, cartridge bag and saddle.*

Right: *A professional buffalo hunter at work. Much of the equipment used by the hunters was bought from the army.*

Below: *A hunting knife.*

"The valley of the Platte is dotted all over with the skeletons of buffalo. Such waste of creatures that God has made for man seems wicked, but every emigrant seems to wish to signalize himself by killing one." Mrs Larkin's Diary

The buffalo, which could be up to 3 metres long, and weigh as much as 1,000 kg, would simply stand there with a dazed expression and then drop to the ground, stone dead. More adventurous hunters might ride into the flank of a stampeding herd, single out a buffalo, and aim for its spine in the hope of felling it with one shot.

Right: *A hunting pouch, a horn powder flask, and two guns. The top one is a shotgun used for small game, and the bottom one is a muzzle-loading rifle for heavier game such as antelope. Below them is a powder keg.*

Above: *An American pheasant.*

Below: *Shooting equipment: a powder flask, bullet mould and gun lock. To make round musket balls for his rifle, Matt Belknap pours lead into the mould through the hole at the top, and waits for it to harden before opening it up again.*

Travellers like the Larkins particularly prized the meat of buffalo cows, the bulls being regarded as too tough and stringy. The hump would be roasted, the tongue braised, and the marrow bones baked in the coals of the campfire. Meat that was not eaten fresh would be preserved by the Indian technique of jerking. Cut into thin strips, it would hang over a smoking fire for half a day, or be dangled from the back of the wagon to dry in the sun. If there was time, the hides would be scraped clean and soaked in a special solution to tan them (turn them into leather).

The earliest overlanders reported seeing the plains black with buffalo, and they lived in fear of a deadly stampede. Even though the buffalo were so plentiful, early overlanders like the Larkins tried to use as much of the buffalo as possible, just as the Indians did. But as overland travel became more common, this changed. Within a few decades, more and more overlanders were killing for "sport" rather than for food, and commercial hunters were killing for the hides. The once vast herds were nearly exterminated and the Indians had lost their traditional hunting forever.

CHILDREN'S ACTIVITIES

For the Larkin children, the journey to Oregon began as one great holiday. "We're going to where the Injuns be!" shouted Abe, when his father told him their plans. Of course, the children still had chores to do each day – milking the cows, carrying water – just as they did back in Indiana. But Abe would not be helping his father with the ploughing, and Rachel and Rebecca would not be doing spinning, quilting and other household chores alongside their mother. Back in Indiana, Rachel, Abe and Rebecca went to school, for most of the winter months at least. Older pupils like Rachel did lessons in grammar and geography from textbooks, and younger ones would work out sums on a slate, practise handwriting or recite in turn from a reader. But there is no time for formal "schooling" on the trail, although Mrs Larkin or one of the other mothers sometimes holds a spelling contest or hears the children recite.

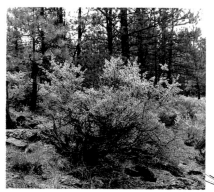

Above: *Rabbitbrush is one plant that the children don't rush to pick – it has a very strong and unpleasant smell!*

Right: *Fir cone.*

The children gather berries, currants and hazelnuts for pies. They look for birds' feathers and pick wild flowers: black-eyed Susans, purple blazing star and the pink prairie rose. Sometimes they find a species they have never seen before, so they save the seeds to plant in Oregon or send to friends back East. But the children soon get tired of the journey. Rebecca complains of either dust or mud, depending on the weather.

Mrs Larkin keeps little Margaret happy by giving her some coloured beads to string together – a difficult task in the bouncing wagon.

Above: *Margaret tries to catch lizards, but they are always too quick for her.*

"Matthew brought me some flowers… Their form and colour resemble the snowball and their perfume the night-blooming jessamine."
Rachel Larkin's Diary

NOONING

I t is midday and the wagons have been rolling along for five hours. The day is hot and the oxen are tired.

Captain Bonner's advance scouts have found a cool stream not far ahead, and he calls a halt. The wagons pull up and the oxen are released, though not unyoked, and the whole party settles down for an hour of rest.

Above:
*Mr and Mrs Larkin
followed the guidebooks'
advice to "lay in a good
supply of school books for the
children" but they are hardly
used on the trail.*

Above: *Overlanders resting beside their wagons at noon.*

*"Mrs Pringle called on me today and very much
admired my bonnet. I promised to give her the pattern
and returned the compliment by admiring her apron."*
Mrs Larkin's Diary

Below: *Abe's fishing gear has a
collapsible rod which is ideal for
travel. He is disappointed by the
lack of fishing on the high plains,
but there are catfish in the slow,
muddy waters of the Big Blue
and trout and salmon in the
rivers of the western
mountains.*

"Nooning" is Mrs Larkin's favourite time of day. The family eat leftovers from breakfast, so she does not have to do any cooking. Margaret, whom she has been carrying on her hip all morning, is allowed to toddle about and play; the older children run off to see their friends in the other wagons; and Mr Larkin leaves for a meeting with Captain Bonner and his council. Mrs Larkin uses the time to relax, rest her weary legs and write in her diary. She notes down the latest gossip on the wagon train and any news she has been able to get of the outside world.

MISHAPS

From 1852 to 1853, almost 90,000 overlanders headed for Oregon and California. The wagon trains, which left the jumping-off points almost daily, often overtook each other. They also met up with "go-backers" who were returning East. These travellers had "seen the elephant" (*see left*), an expression meaning that they had experienced the hardships of life in the West and decided they could not put up with them. Besides the weariness of months of travel, the overlanders had many other problems: even if the driver was as good as Mr Larkin, any wagon could break down, and the oxen could become sick or exhausted (*see below*).

Above: *Crossing the Plains, 1851. Painting by Charles Nahl.*

"Alkali water" killed many oxen. This water was full of chemical salts left behind as the lakes dried out in the hot weather. An ox that had drunk this water might be saved if chunks of bacon and swigs of vinegar could be forced down its throat to stop the salts burning its insides. Rough ground and desert sands were also a hazard for oxen, as they often led to lameness and sore feet. The remedy for this was to put the ox in booties made of rawhide.

Above: *There were other hazards besides sick oxen. A broken wheel was almost irreplaceable. Few wagon trains had time to wait while a new wheel was made out of a discarded table top or some other piece of quality furniture.*

Right: *A "brake" made of strong rope stopped the wheels turning.*

"There is no end to the wagons, buggies, yokes, chains, etc. that are lying all along this road, and many the poor horses, mules, oxen, cows, etc. that are lying dead in these mountains." Mrs Larkin's Diary

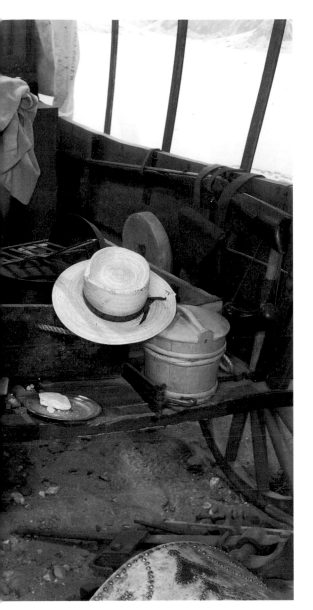

Broken axles were looked on as a matter of course. Nearly every wagon started out with at least one spare, to avoid a detour of miles in search of a tree large enough to be made into a replacement.

The iron tyres on the wagon wheels sometimes became loose as the wooden wheels shrank in the dry desert air, and they had to be held in place by wedges.

Left: *Almost every overlander had to abandon some valued objects, ranging from cook-stoves and furniture to barrels of bacon and boxes of books in order to lighten their load. One overlander even spotted an abandoned diving bell!*

Difficult Terrain

Mountain slopes and steep hills presented a challenge, even to the most experienced driver. It was relatively easy to go uphill, as the oxen were used to pulling, and they could be double-teamed. If the going was very hard, a makeshift windlass could be set up: an empty wagon was staked onto the hilltop, leaving one set of wheels running free. A strong rope was then tied to the axle of the free wheels and lowered to the wagon below. Men and oxen would slowly turn the wheels, reeling the wagon up the hill like a fish at the end of a line. Going downhill was more difficult, as oxen were not used to braking. Rope "brakes" could be used to lock the wheels, but this did not always stop the wagon sliding down the hill and being damaged. Even the gently rolling plains could cause problems for an inexperienced driver, as the top-heavy wagons tipped over easily.

Left: *Tool box for wagon repairs.*

CROSSING A RIVER

The wagon trail followed the course of rivers because they provided water and grass. However, they were difficult to cross. By the time the Larkins made their journey, there were many ferries which made crossing safer and easier. But heavy traffic on the trail sometimes created delays of several days and prices were high.

If there was no bridge or ferry, or if the overlander did not have enough money to use them, he could drive his wagon with his

family inside across the river or stream at its shallowest point, moving steadily so that the wagon did not get bogged down in shifting sand.

Mr Larkin, whose guidebooks were out-of-date, had not expected the extra expense, so he usually makes the livestock swim across and puts only the wagon on the ferry. He is annoyed by the delay of waiting for the ferry, but Mrs Larkin is delighted to have a chance to do the laundry. Lacking firewood, she and Rachel must make do with cold water and lots of harsh, strong soap. The soap is homemade, from a liquid called lye which was got from ashes and animal fat.

After a thorough rubbing, the clothing is rinsed, wrung out, and hung on bushes to dry. If there are no bushes, it may simply be worn wet.

"Mother and I burnt our arms very badly while washing. They were red and swollen and painful as though scalded with boiling water". Rachel Larkin's Diary

Above: *Shallow places to cross, or fords, are not always easy to find. Hidden boulders or quicksand could wreck a wagon, like the one abandoned here, or it might overturn in a tricky current.*

Below: *If the water was too deep to drive across, there was no alternative but to tow the wagon across with the swimming cattle, as this painting shows.*
Mr Larkin usually asks Matt to ride ahead of the wagon and look out for any dangers.

The Thomas Gilcrease Institute of American History and Art, Tulsa, Oklahoma

Disaster

R umours of disaster spread quickly, and the Larkins would have heard of the terrible fates of overlanders such as the Donner Party. This wagon train was full of rich families who left their jumping-off point at the end of May 1846, a month late because they had been kitting out wagons with fancy things. They exhausted their oxen trying to catch up with the rest of the overlanders, and took a short-cut recommended in Lansford Hasting's guidebook. The author wanted to make the route seem easy, but he had not even tried it himself! Travelling only two or three kilometres a day in the grassless salt desert, the party were forced to abandon most of their animals. By the time they reached the foothills of the Sierra Nevada, snow had blocked the mountain passes and it was too late to turn back. They had to spend the winter there, in rough log cabins. By mid-December the party was starving and 17 of them tried to cross the mountains to get help (*see above left*). Seven of this party made it to Sutter's Fort and a rescue operation was started. After two failed attempts, a rescue party finally reached them in April 1847. Only 47 of the original 81 people were alive. Many had survived only by eating their dead companions.

The Donner Party was not the only one to run into trouble. Stephen Meek persuaded his party to take a new route in order to avoid the Blue Mountains. They ended up lost, with no grass or water. Meek went ahead by himself and managed to reach the Columbia River. A rescue party was organized, but they found that 75 people had already died.

If such disasters were rare, it was because overlanders learned from others' mistakes. Virginia Reed, a survivor from the Donner party, had some good advice for anyone thinking of making the journey: "Never take no cut offs and hurry along as fast as you can."

Above: *Lansford Hasting's misleading guidebook.*

Stopping at a Fort

Before setting out from Independence, the Larkins followed the guidebooks' instructions closely, as they wanted to have enough supplies for the whole trip. However, not all emigrants were so careful, and even those who had packed properly often found they needed extra supplies, so they were glad of forts and trading posts along the way.

Right: A painting of Fort Laramie and the surrounding Indian village by Alfred Jacob Miller.

Left: A photographer has set up shop at the fort, and people have pictures taken to send to their relatives.

Fort Laramie

The Larkins' party has arrived at Fort Laramie, which by 1853 had become a bustling trading post. It was originally established by the American Fur Company in 1834 to buy animal pelts brought in by "mountain men" and Indian trappers to fur traders (*see opposite page*). By the 1840s, the numbers of overlanders had grown and more money could be made from selling them goods and offering them much-needed services such as a post office, a hospital and a blacksmith than from selling furs.

Many people felt that soldiers should be stationed along the wagon trails to protect overlanders against attacks by Indians, and by the 1850s, 90 per cent of the US Army was stationed in the West. The army bought Fort Laramie from the American Fur Company in 1849 and it became the first and most important of a string of military garrisons. At Fort Laramie, the sutler, or army provisioner, who supplied the troops with food from his shop also sold goods to the overlanders.

Above: *The sign outside the sutler's store boasts that it stocks "all articles a man wants in civilized countries or on the plains".*

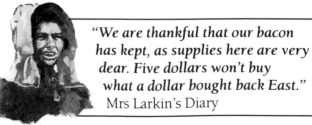

"We are thankful that our bacon has kept, as supplies here are very dear. Five dollars won't buy what a dollar bought back East."
Mrs Larkin's Diary

34

Fort Laramie a Sublette's Fort near the Nebraska a Platte River

Although the sight of the cavalry's blue coats made the overlanders feel safe, the army was not really very good at protecting them. Reports of problems with Indians could take days to reach a fort, and sometimes the cavalry's response would be to attack the wrong Indians. This caused more fighting and made the Indians mistrustful of both the army and the overlanders. The government's Indian agents, who arranged peace treaties with various Indian tribes in exchange for annual payments, were far more effective than the soldiers. However, the army and the Indians were not completely hostile to one another: villages of Indians, eager for trade with the overlanders, usually encircled the walls of the forts.

Right: *Some of the furs traded in the early days at Fort Laramie: deer, red fox, ermine, river otter and buffalo.*

Left: *An infantryman in uniform.*

Above: *A cavalryman's saddle, curry combs and canteen.*

Right: *A soldier's winter overcoat and belt with a powder pouch and bullet bag and pistol. Cavalrymen usually carried pairs of pistols in holsters like the ones shown here, slung over the fronts of their saddles.*

35

A SPECIAL DAY

O nly rarely did the Larkins and their company take time off for a celebration. Even Sunday, the Sabbath for these normally religious people, would be spent like any other day, unless they encountered a travelling

Above: *The family Bible.*

preacher. People said, "There's no Sunday West of Kansas". Weddings, however, did call for special activity. The couple's friends would spend the wedding night pushing and jostling their wagon, shooting off guns and banging on kettles. This was called a "chivaree". Overlanders tended to marry young, especially the girls. It was unusual for a girl not to be married by the age of 16.

Right: *Preparations for the Independence Day celebrations.*

Only one special day is regularly mentioned in the overlanders' diaries: the Fourth of July – American Independence Day. The Larkins' company are pleased because they have reached Independence Rock, so named by a group of early travellers who reached it on Independence Day. This means that, despite the rainy weather, they are right on schedule. They spend a few days on the grassy banks of the Sweetwater River, grazing their oxen and celebrating their good fortune.

The Fourth of July Feast
The sideboards of the wagons are laden with roasted antelope, sage hen and rabbit; several kinds of fresh bread; baked beans, rice, and, as a special treat, Irish potatoes and pickled cucumbers brought all the way from Missouri. To drink, there is coffee, tea and lemonade made of sugar, water, citric acid and a few drops of essence of lemon. Over a dozen sorts of cakes and pies are spread out for dessert, and some long-hoarded chocolate is given to the children.

Matt and Rachel join a group of young people who climb Independence Rock

Above: *It was a tradition for the travellers to sign their names on Independence Rock.*

to write their own names and to look for the names of friends. Meanwhile, Mrs Larkin and the other women have decided that, to celebrate properly, they need an American flag. One of them has some scraps of blue cloth, another has red, and another white. By the time the party begins, the American flag flies from a makeshift flagpole in the middle of the wagon circle. Many of the company are dressed up in costume. Rachel is decked out as "Lady Liberty", but most of the young people are dressed as Indians. The "Indians" perform "war dances" to the delight of the crowd.

There is a contest to see which of the children can best remember the words of the Declaration of Independence from their school days back East, with the winner to receive the last precious piece of chocolate. The "official" party closes with three cheers for America (Oregon Territory in particular) and a five-gun salute, but the dancing and revelling go on late into the night.

Right: *Pen-box, inkwell and spectacles. Steel tipped pens began replacing quills in the late 1820s.*

As always, Mrs Larkin writes a detailed account of the celebration in her diary. Many overlanders kept diaries, and a lot of them still survive. Some, like Mr Larkin's, have short entries: "June 20. Up Platte River. Good road. Made 21 mi. June 29. Up same. Overtook Capt. Tutherew's Company. Made 15 mi." Others, like Mrs Larkin's and Rachel's, contain more interesting information.

SICKNESS & MEDICINES

O f nearly 300,000 emigrants who headed West between 1840 and 1860, around 30,000, or one in ten, died along the way. Some diaries speak of practically nothing but death and burial. Accidents accounted for the deaths of some of the overlanders. Diary accounts tell of little children falling out of wagons and being crushed beneath the wheels; of people being shot by night guards who mistook them for Indians trying to steal their livestock; and of men being swept away and drowned when they tried to herd their cattle across raging rivers.

Left: *A wooden tombstone like this was unusual. Most graves were simply mounds of earth.*

Above: Prairie Burial, *c. 1848. Painting by William Tylee Ranney. Even if a person was in the best of health, a serious attack of cholera could kill them in a single day.*

"July 11. Passed 15 graves. Made 13 mi. July 12. Passed 5 graves. Saw 8 dead cattle. Made 10 mi."
Mr Larkin's Diary

However, the most common cause of death on the trail was disease: measles, typhoid, mountain fever, the "bloody flux" or dysentery, and above all the dreaded cholera. Asiatic cholera, carried by rats on ships, arrived in American port cities in late 1848 and 1849, and from there it spread to places with poor water supplies and bad plumbing. Even cities such as St Louis lost a tenth of their population. The wagon trains, which were camping and watering every day with no proper toilets, in the same campsites as all the previous trains, were particularly hard hit by the disease.

Like most overlanders, the Larkins have a variety of medicines: laudanum (tincture of opium) and camphor for cholera, hartshorne for snake bites, citric acid for scurvy, castor oil for bowel disorders, borax and alum for boils and sores, whiskey and various dried herbs for everything else.

Doctors
If someone was very ill, the overlanders might try to summon a doctor. Often travelling by wagon train themselves, doctors advertised their services and let people know where they were by posting notices on the "roadside telegraph". Their fees varied considerably. Some took payment only for medicines, while others charged a fee for visiting the patient. Typical charges might be $2.00 for

seeing a cholera victim and $5.00 for an amputation or for setting a broken limb.

But even doctors knew little about the cause and prevention of cholera. It was not until 1865 that Louis Pasteur demonstrated that germs cause diseases like cholera. The doctors did know that dirty water was associated with the disease, but they did not realize that boiling the water would kill the deadly germs. It is very lucky for the Larkins that they like to drink strong boiled coffee with every meal. This makes them much less likely to catch cholera.

Even overlanders who remained fairly healthy, like the Larkins, still had to put up with the never-ending nuisance of mosquito bites. It was common for people to be bitten so many times that their blood stopped being able to clot.

Above:
An advertisement for cholera remedies.

Left: *A portable medical case.*

Right: *Quinine was used to treat the disease malaria, which overlanders caught from mosquito bites.*

"So many of our company have died of the cholera that I cannot recount all their names. The burials have been at night on account of Indians robbing the graves for wearing apparel. The graves are concealed by building a fire on them and then driving the entire train of wagons over them when we break camp in the morning."
Mrs Larkin's Diary

39

Right: *Setting up camp for the night.*

Above:
*Mrs Larkin decides
not to light a lantern. Her candles
have to last until she arrives in
Oregon and can make more.*

SETTING UP CAMP

R ain and heavy trail traffic has made it hard to find good
campsites this year, and sometimes the Larkins' wagon train
has travelled late into the night before reaching a suitable
place. Today, however, Captain Bonner's advance scouts have had
no trouble. At 6 pm the bugle sounds. Captain Bonner lays out some
stakes to help him guide the train into a neat circle. He is so accurate
that the last wagon closes the circle perfectly. The operation has
taken only ten minutes.

Mr Larkin and Matt Belknap unyoke the oxen and drive them to
pasture near a waterhole. Then they water the horses. Finally, just
inside the wagon circle, they set up the little wall tent in which
Rachel, Abe and Rebecca will sleep. Mr and Mrs Larkin and Margaret
will sleep on featherbeds inside the wagon. Matt will sleep in the
open, though if it rains he will roll under the wagon.

*"O dear, I do so want to get there! It is now
two months since we have slept in a house. If only I
could be set down at home with all the folks…"*
Mrs Larkin's Diary

Above: *Mrs Larkin cooks dinner
for her family in iron pots.
The cups and plates are made
of tin.*

40

Above: *Hobbles like the one shown are used to tie the horses to the wagon for the night.*

Right: *A folding camp chair makes dining much more comfortable.*

ENTERTAINMENT

On the high plains the overlanders went to bed early since there was little fuel for fires. But elsewhere, they gathered together to chat about the day's travel. Some men played dice or cards, but others thought that gambling was sinful. Some people even thought that playing chess was wicked.

Whiskey is also frowned upon, although many overlanders, especially gold miners, did drink. On the Larkins' wagon train, it is used "for medicinal purposes only". Dancing and singing, however, are enjoyed by everyone. Songs about home, love and death are popular, as are funny songs like "Oh Susanna".

It is midnight when the fiddler stops playing, but the Larkins are already in bed and asleep. Matt Belknap, on the watch, is still awake. He gazes up at the stars and thinks about Oregon.

The family's dinner will be cornbread and beans, fried meat and gravy – the basic diet of the overlander. But there will be warm milk, fresh from the cow, to drink, and Mrs Larkin and Rebecca have found enough berries to make a pie, which will be baked in the old dutch oven.

The men of the party have been divided into three companies, each split into four watches. One company has to guard the wagon train each night, the first watch waking members of the second watch, and so on through the night. It is just 8 pm when the first watch takes up its duties.

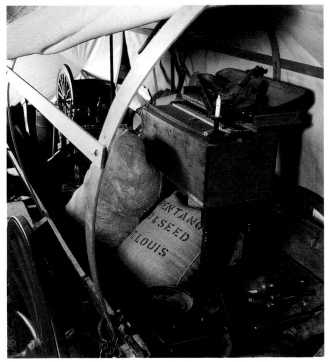

Above: *The Larkins' party is lucky enough to have a melodeon, or American organ, as well as fiddles and harmonicas. They plan to have a "cotillion" or square dance with visitors from a nearby wagon train.*

OREGON AT LAST

The Larkins arrive in Oregon City on September 10, 1853, four months after leaving Independence and nearly five months after leaving Indiana. On the last stages of their journey two of their oxen died and had to be replaced by cows, but they themselves have all survived to see "civilization" again. They spend a few days shopping for food and catching up on the latest news of Oregon and the world. Although prices are higher than in St Louis, they are at least lower than on the trail.

Above: *Oregon City as it looked in 1848. Painting by Henry J. Warre.*

Left: *Building a log cabin.*

Below: *Tin wash-tubs hang on the outside of the Larkins' new cabin.*

Soon the Larkins are on the move again, this time for the short journey to the less developed regions of the upper Willamette Valley (*see page 4*) to claim their new land. No one is surprised when Matt Belknap asks Rachel to marry him, and she accepts.

As a married couple, they too will be given their own land under the terms of the 1850 Donation Land Act (*see page 6*).

Left: *The* Daily Portland Times *advertises livestock sales, saloons and job opportunities.*

42

Mrs Larkin can be proud of. A new stove will provide heat, and a flat-iron will allow her to press her treasured fancy aprons and calico frocks.

Bountiful crops of grain and hops – as well as clean mountain water – will provide the raw materials for brewing beer. The Larkins expect to do well in Oregon – a land not exactly flowing with milk and honey but still very prosperous.

Above: *Mrs Larkin will have little chance to spin in Oregon, as there are very few sheep. A few women tried spinning hair from wolves, but as these animals cannot be fleeced while alive, it was not very practical. Most people relied either on store-bought cloth or wore buckskin like the mountain men.*

Left: *Supplies carried in the wagon are at last stored in the Larkins' new log cabin. Included are an iron wood-burning stove, canteens, irons, and pots and pans. There is also an accordion and the latest edition of a local newspaper.*

Above right: *A candle mould. Although there is not much beeswax, there is plenty of tallow, so Mrs Larkin can make candles.*

Below: *Mrs Larkin uses a basket and bottles as a pantry.*

Settling In

With no summer crops to live on and little money left, the Larkins have a hard first winter in Oregon, but with their neighbours' help, they survive. Mr Larkin builds a log cabin. Even the chimney is wooden, but fortunately it is well plastered with mud on the inside to reduce the risk of fire. Mr Larkin cannot afford window glass yet: that costs $6.00 (£3.50) for a small box. Neither can he construct a proper shingle roof: that would take too much time. Instead, he puts up a rough frame and covers it with canvas from the wagon top. A buffalo hide serves as the door. The wagon box is broken up for furniture. The Larkins' "Hoosier Home" has become part of their new home in Oregon. Within a few years, it will be transformed into something that even

"I am thankful that we have at last reached Oregon. The land is better than we had hoped, and our prospects are bright." Mr Larkin

THE WAGON IN TIME

T he Larkins travelled from Indiana to Oregon in 1853. Here are some of the things that took place in the United States and around the world before, during and after the time that the Larkins made their journey.

1800 Population of the USA recorded as 5,308,483.

1803 The USA pays France $15,000,000 for the lands between the Mississippi and the Rocky Mountains, thus doubling the size of the nation.

1804-1806 The Lewis and Clark Expedition explores the upper Missouri and Oregon territory.

1805-1807 Zebulon Pike searches for the source of the Mississippi and explores the Rocky Mountains.

1807 Engineer Robert Fulton develops the first practical steamboat.

1811 John Jacob Astor establishes a trading post in Oregon.

1812-1814 War between the USA and Great Britain.

1816 The state of Indiana is admitted to the union.

1818 The USA and Great Britain agree to joint occupancy of Oregon country.

1819 The USA buys Florida from Spain.

1820 Death of frontiersman and American folk hero Daniel Boone at age 85.

1821-1824 Wars of independence end Spanish colonial rule in Mexico and South America.

1828 The first American railroad, the Baltimore and Ohio, begins operation. Andrew Jackson, advocate of Western expansion, is elected President of the USA.

1830 Joseph Smith founds the Mormon Church (Latter Day Saints).
Congress passes the Indian Removal Act, giving President Jackson the power to remove Native Americans from the East to lands west of the Mississippi.

1832 *Godey's Lady's Book* begins publication in the USA. A popular magazine, it introduced women to the latest fashions and literature.

1833 John Deere patents the steel plough, which, unlike the older cast iron plough, can turn over the heavy turf of the Western prairies.

1834 Cyrus McCormick patents the reaper.

1835 Samuel Colt patents his six-shooter revolver.

1836 The Lone Star Republic (now Texas) becomes independent from Mexico.
Marcus and Narcissa Whitman establish a Methodist mission in Oregon Country.

1837 Accession of Queen Victoria to the throne of Great Britain.

1838 French inventor Louis Daguerre develops the first practical photographic process, producing "daguerreotypes".

1842-1845 John Frémont maps the West.

1843 First wagon train crosses to Oregon.
Samuel Morse's electromagnetic telegraph operates between Washington and Baltimore.

1844 James K Polk elected President of the United States on a slogan of "All of Oregon or War".

1845 The Lone Star Republic enters the union as the state of Texas. In his *Democratic Review* John L O'Sullivan writes of the United States' "Manifest Destiny" to expand across the continent.

1846 The Bear Flag Republic (now California) becomes independent from Mexico.
The Donner Party disaster.

1847 Oregon Boundary Treaty divides the territory between the USA and Great Britain. Marcus and Narcissa Whitman and 12 other settlers are massacred by a group of *Cayuse* Indians at their mission in Oregon. Brigham Young leads the Mormons from Nauvoo, Illinois, to Utah.

1848 War with Mexico results in the Mexican Cession of California and the Southwest to the USA.
Gold is discovered in California, leading to the 1849-50 Gold Rush.

1850 The Donation Land Act is passed in the USA.
Irish immigration to the USA after the Potato Famine reaches 160,000 per year.
Harper's Monthly begins publication in the USA, offering English novels in serial form and illustrated articles about the West.

1852 Harriet Beecher Stowe's novel *Uncle Tom's Cabin* attacks slavery.

1853 The USA acquires southern New Mexico and Arizona from Mexico by the Gadsden Purchase.

The Larkin family emigrate to Oregon.

1854 The Kansas–Nebraska Act formally opens these territories to white settlement and sparks new national debate on slavery.

1859 First oil well, in Pennsylvania, leads to the development of the petroleum industry.
Silver is discovered in Nevada.

1860 First Pony Express delivers letters from St Louis, Missouri, to Sacramento,

California, in 10 days.
Population of the USA reaches 31,500,000.
Abraham Lincoln is elected President of the USA.

1861-1865 The American Civil War.

1861 Telegraph line completed between San Francisco and St Louis.
Emperor Alexander II of Russia emancipates the serfs.

1862 Homestead Act encourages settlement of unoccupied western lands.

1863 Lincoln's Emancipation Proclamation frees the slaves.

1864 Death of Stephen Foster, composer of "Old Kentucky Home" and "The Camptown Races", at age 38.

1865 Lincoln assassinated.
French scientist Louis Pasteur publishes his "germ theory" of disease.

1866 First successful transatlantic telegraph cable.

1867 The USA buys Alaska from Russia for $7,200,000.
Swedish inventor Alfred Nobel develops dynamite.
George Henry Hammond produces the first railway refrigerator car.

1869 The first American trans-continental railroad is completed.
The first professional baseball team is organized, in Cincinnati.

1872 The first US national park is established as the Yellowstone National Park.

1874 Barbed wire is patented. Economical fencing and the introduction of "winter wheat" encourages the development of farming on the Great Plains.
Alexander Graham Bell demonstrates the telephone.

1875 Gold Rush onto *Sioux* lands leads to the Battle of Little Big Horn ("Custer's Last Stand") in 1876.

1877 Chief Joseph of the *Nez Perce* surrenders to the US Cavalry.
Thomas A Edison invents the gramophone.

1879 Thomas A Edison demonstrates the electric light.

1882 The first commercial electricity system is put in operation in New York City.

1883 The first ten-storey "skyscraper" is built in Chicago.

1884 American inventor Hiram Maxim perfects the machine gun.

1886 First manufacture of Coca-Cola.

1887 Golden Jubilee of Queen Victoria.

1888 Scotsman John Dunlop invents the pneumatic tyre.
American George Eastman perfects the hand camera.

1889 Two million acres of Indian Territory (Oklahoma) are opened to white homesteaders.

1890 Battle of Wounded Knee, ending the Western "Indian Wars".
Population of the USA reaches 63,000,000 as 450,000 immigrants arrive annually.

GLOSSARY

Bloomers Full, loose trousers, gathered round the ankle, which were introduced by the American social reformer Amelia Jenks Bloomer in 1850 because they were more practical for women to wear than long, trailing skirts.

Brave An Indian warrior. Among the Native Americans of the Plains, boys had to prove their bravery and strength at hunting and warfare in order to be called braves, and they competed with each other for the top position. The highest ranking braves of the tribe were the chiefs, who were highly honoured, as were the shamans or "medicine men", who had spiritual power. While young boys were taught to become braves, girls were taught home-making skills like sewing by their mothers and the other women of the tribe, who were called "squaws."

Buckskin Soft leather made from the hide of deer or elk, so named because a male deer is called a "buck".

Buffalo Robe A blanket made from the whole hide of a buffalo, tanned with the hair still on it in order to give extra warmth.

Calico A brightly printed cotton fabric.

Cholera A short-lasting, often fatal infection caused by drinking or eating water, milk or food contaminated with bacteria. The symptoms are diarrhoea, vomiting and stomach pains, followed by collapse from loss of water and salt.

Dutch Oven A heavy cast-iron pot with a tightly-fitting cover. When heaped with coals, it can be used for baking as well as for stewing.

Dysentery A common and highly infectious trail disease whose symptoms include fatigue, nausea and diarrhoea followed by loss of water and salt.

Emigrant A person who leaves their native country or region to live elsewhere. The early overlanders were called emigrants because they left the settled parts of the United States to go and live in lands in the West which were only just being acquired by the US government.

Forty-Niner A person who went to California looking for gold during the 1849 gold rush.

Gingham A cotton fabric, often with a striped or checked pattern.

Independence Day In the seventeenth century, Great Britain founded 13 colonies on the eastern coast of America. The people who lived there did not want to be controlled by Britain, and this led to the American War of Independence. On the 4th of July 1776, representatives from each of the 13 colonies signed the Declaration of Independence of the American Colonies from Great Britain. The colonists, led by George Washington, finally defeated the British in 1781, and in 1783 Britain recognized American Independence and the 13 colonies were re-named the United States of America. The 4th of July is known as "Independence Day", and it is the oldest national holiday in the United States.

Indian Agent A representative of the US government who served as an ambassador to one or more Indian tribes.

Johnnycake A type of bread made of cornmeal mixed with salt and water or milk, which could be either baked in a pan or fried on a griddle.

Mormon A member of the Church of Jesus Christ of Latter-Day Saints, which was a religious group founded in the US by Joseph Smith in 1830. After being driven out of their homes in the East because of religious intolerance, many Mormons, under the leadership of Brigham Young, emigrated to the place that would, in 1846, become the State of Utah.

Mountain Fever A general name given to several diseases which emigrants sometimes caught on the western parts of the Oregon Trail. The symptoms included chills, fever and extreme fatigue. Mountain fever was weakening, but rarely fatal.

Mountain Men Professional trappers of animals for fur who hunted in the mountain ranges. As more and more emigrants came west, these men were often paid to serve as wagon train guides or "pilots".

Native American A term used for the tribes still living today in the United States. The overlanders would have called these people "Indians".

Penny Press Publishing companies that sold cheap mini-novels and short stories, which were often very sensational.

Pilot Bread Also known as "hardtack", this was a hard biscuit made from flour and water. As it would keep for a long time, it was commonly used for long journeys by both land and sea.

Prairie The wide, rolling land of the Missouri–Mississippi valley. It has almost no trees, but very deep and rich soil and enough rain for good crops of grain. On its west side, the prairie merges with the high plains, where a lack of rainfall makes the land more suitable for grazing animals than for growing crops.

Rawhide Untanned leather, usually without hair, that has been cured by being stretched and dried.

Scurvy People get this disease when they do not have enough ascorbic acid, which is found in foods such as lemons and limes. The symptoms include loose teeth and bleeding gums.

Tallow Melted animal fat. It was usually made into candles or mixed up with grease and used to keep the wagon wheels running smoothly.

Typhoid A highly infectious and often fatal disease caused by bacteria. The symptoms are fever, diarrhoea, headaches and, in the later stages, confusion and haemorrhaging of blood.

INDEX

Please note: references to the Larkin family are to be found under the headings 'father', 'mother', and 'children'.

PLACES TO VISIT

The following museums have displays on aspects of life on the wagon trail:

THE AMERICAN MUSEUM
Claverton Manor
Bath BA2 7BD
Tel: 01225-460503

ASHBURTON MUSEUM
1 West Street
Ashburton, Devon
Telephone number not available

HORNIMAN MUSEUM
100 London Road
London SE23 EPQ
Tel: 0181-699 1872

IPSWICH MUSEUM
High Street
Ipswich
Tel: 01473-213761

BRITISH MUSEUM
Great Russell Street
London WClB 3DG
Tel: 0171-437 2224

PITT RlVERS MUSEUM
South Parks Road
Oxford OX1 3PP
Tel: 01865-270949

MAIDSTONE MUSEUM AND ART GALLERY
St Faith's Street
Maidstone, Kent ME14 1LH
Tel: 01622-754497

Acknowledgements

Breslich & Foss would like to thank Bob Boyd and Jack Cooper from The High Desert museum, Helen and John Erickson, Adair Law from the Oregon Historical Society, Maggie Harris from the Jefferson National Expansion Memorial, Linda Morgese from the Hackley school Library, and Francia White for their assistance.

Picture Credits

The Anschutz Collection Photo: James O Milmoe: p.38 (top centre).

State of California Depatment of Parks and Recreation: p.35 (centre).

California State Library, Sacramento, California: p.5 (top), p 33 (top left).

Museum of Church History and Art, Salt Lake City: p.15 (bottom left).

The Denver Public library, Western History Depatment: p.8 (centre left), p.29 (top centre).

Helen Erickson: p.11 (top center), p.17 (top right).

Fort Lamie p.34 (centre right).

The High Desert Museum, Bend, Oregon: p.7 (bottom right), p.8 (bottom left), p.10 (bottom right), p.11 (bottom centre), p.12 (top left), p.13 (bottom left), p.16 (bottom left), p.17 (bottom centre), p.18 (bottom, top right), p.19 (top right), p.20 (centre left), p.21 (top right), p.26 (bottom left), p.27 (top right, bottom left), p.29 (bottom centre), p.30-31 (centre), p.31 (centre right, bottom left, bottom centre), p.34 (centre left), p.35 (bottom right), p.37 (centre right, centre left), p.40 (top left, bottom right), p.41 (bottom left), p.42 (bottom right), p.42-43 (top centre), p.43 (top right, bottom right).

The Huntingdon Library, San Marino, California p.9 (top left), p.30 (top left), p.32 (left centre), p.37 (top centre).

James K Polk Memorial Association, Columbia, Tennessee: p.5 (bortom left).

Jefferson National Expansion Historical Association, St Louis, Missouri: p.5 (top right), p.10 (left), p.10-11 (centre) p.11 (centre right), p.13 (bottom centre), p.l4 (bottom left), p.14-15 (bottom centre), p.15 (top right), p.19 (bottom right), p.22 (bottom centre, bottom right), p.23 (bottom right), p.25 (top right, bottom right), p.26 (top left, centre left), p.27 (centre right), p.28 (centre left, bottom right), p.35 (centre right, centre left), p.39 (centre right).

Joslyn Art Museum, Omaha, Nebraska: p.34 (top centre).

The Los Angeles Athletic Club Art Collection Photo: Lawrence Reynolds: p.16 (top centre).

National Archives: p.32 (top centre).

Museum of New Mexico: p.40 (top centre).

Collection of the New-York Historical Society: p.39 (top centre).

The Oakland Museum History Department: p.18 (top left), p.38 (top left).

Oregon Historical Society, Portland, Oregon p.6 (centre lett, centre right) p.7 (centre), p.8 (bottom centre), p.9 (bottom left), p.13 (centre right), p.14-15 (centre), p.16 (top left), p.20-21 (top centre), p.22 (centre left), p.24 (top right, bottom left), p.26-27 (bottom centre), p.28-29 (centre), p.33 (centre right), p.36 (centre left), p.39 (bottom left), p.41 (top left, bottom right), p.42 (bottom left), p.43 (top left).

Stanford University Museum of Art, Gift of Jane L. Stanford: p.30 (centre left).

The Thomas Gilcrease Institute of American History and Art: p.32 (bottom centre).

Walters Art Gallery, Baltimore: p.21 (centre left).